MONEY SENSE &
NONSENSE

OTHER MATTERS OF FACT BOOKS

MATTERS OF
FACT

MONEY SENSE
&
NONSENSE

IRENA CHALMERS

AN IRENA CHALMERS BOOK

Longmeadow Press

**PREPARED FOR LONGMEADOW PRESS BY
IRENA CHALMERS BOOKS, INC.**

MANAGING EDITOR: **Carlotta Kerwin**
ASSISTANT TO THE EDITOR: **David Chestnut**
COPY EDITOR: **Linda Stern**
PICTURE EDITOR: **Lisa Sorensen**

———————

COVER DESIGN: **Karen Skelton**
ART DIRECTION AND DESIGN: **Helene Berinsky**

TYPESETTING: **Pica Graphics, Monsey, New York**

———————

MONEY SENSE & NONSENSE

Published by Longmeadow Press, 201 High Ridge Road, Stamford, Connecticut 06904. No part of this book may be reproduced or used in any form or by any means, electronic or mechanical, including photocopying, recording, or by an information storage and retrieval system, without permission in writing from the publisher.

ISBN 0-681-40693-3

Printed in the United States of America

0 9 8 7 6 5 4 3 2 1

CONTENTS

PICTURE CREDITS

p. 8, 23, 32, 36, 62 Cartoons by Mort Gerberg 11, 27, 30, 40, 61 Culver Pictures, Inc. 15 From *Money: From Cowrie Shells to Credit Cards*, edited by Joe Cribb, British Museum Publications 17, 33 Courtesy of the Federal Reserve Bank of New York 19, 44 Illustration by Isadore Seltzer 22 Photograph by August Sander: *Laborer*, 1927, The New York Public Library Picture Collection 24–25 Courtesy of the Federal Reserve Bank of Atlanta 26 Illustration by Richard Rosenblum 33 Courtesy of the Federal Reserve Bank of New York 34 The Lester Glassner Collection 58–59 Museum of the City of New York

PICTURE CONSULTANT: ILENE CHERNA BELLOVIN

CHAPTER 1

MONEY TALKS

Consider, if you will, the following: "folding money," "front money," "in the money," "hard currency," "a license to print money," "mad money," "make money hand over fist," "on the money," "money from home," "put one's money where one's mouth is," "smart money," "throw money at something," and suddenly you discover that money talks!

DOWN ON THE FARM

The "well-heeled," who are "living high on the hog," may "spare a dime" for those who are "as poor as church mice" and unable to "keep the wolf from the door."

MONEY EATS

Most of the world's population needs money primarily to obtain food. It is not surprising then that many of the synonyms for money are actually words for food: "small potatoes," "dough," "bread," "gravy," "nest egg," "chicken feed," "bread and butter," and "peanuts."

Never ask of money spent
Where the spender thinks it went
Nobody was ever meant
To remember or invent
What he did with every cent.

ROBERT FROST

NICE GUYS FINISH LAST

Many "fat cats" achieve success by "making a killing" one way or another. This is how they get to live "on easy street."

WITH THIS RING

Undoubtedly the most painful way to obtain money is to marry for it.

WHAT'LL IT BE?

When it comes to a choice between love or money, most over the age of puberty will settle for money. When we make vows of eternal love for richer or poorer, we would, on the whole, prefer richer.

Money may be the husk of many things, but not the kernel. It brings you food, but not appetite; medicine, but not health; acquaintances, but not friends; servants, but not faithfulness; days of joy, but not peace or happiness.

HENRIK IBSEN

IT'S A WAY TO
ESTABLISH INDEPENDENCE

Money has three uses. It is a means of exchange for goods and services; it is a tangible means of establishing a value or price; and, lastly, it is a collectible. The more you collect, the more people are nice to you.

When a fellow says it hain't the money but the principle o' the thing, it's th' money.

ABE MARTIN

IF YOU HAVE TO ASK

Money magazine made some undercover inquiries concerning sexual preference. It seems 47 percent of the men responding said they enjoy sex more than money. Only 26 percent of women said they preferred sex to money.

They said that knowledge is power. I used to think so, but I now know that they mean money.

BYRON

SIGNING IS OFF

J. I. Rodale, in his definitive work, *The Synonym Finder,* tells us that "credit" is a noun. Further reading reveals it is synonymous with "trustworthiness, faithfulness, integrity, honor, rectitude, probity, veracity, honesty, good faith, credibility, reliability, dependability, and solvency." Let's try to remember to tell the credit companies that when they doubt us.

If you would lose a troublesome visitor, lend him money.

OSCAR WILDE

HOW BEAUTIFUL IS
THE MONEY TREE

Parents are forever reminding their children that money "does not grow on trees." Carrying the image of growing things another step, they say money is the "root of all evil." What we really mean though is that other people's money is evil. If it fell into our pockets, it would instantly become good.

Though mothers and fathers give us life, it is money alone which preserves it.

IHARA SAIKAKU

DEFINING MONEY

- Mr. Money-Bags is a person of age with deep pockets.
- A money lender does so carefully.
- A moneymaker, while not actually making money, ends up with it nevertheless.
- A moneywort is a creeping perennial with rounded, opposite leaves and yellow flowers.

I've never been poor, only broke. Being poor is a frame of mind. Being broke is only a temporary situation.

MIKE TODD

CHAPTER 2

LEGAL TENDER

Money, or more specifically, coinage, can trace its roots back at least 2,500 years through the media of gold, silver, and copper. Though these were not the only forms of money, they were, and still are, the most widely used.

CENTS AND SENSIBILITY

Fifty years after his death, Abraham Lincoln was honored again. His face has been engraved on every cent minted since 1909. We are in touch with Mr. Lincoln constantly, but we don't see much of Woodrow Wilson these days. His likeness is on the $100,000 bill. Most people use checks for sums as large as $100,000.

SITTING PRETTY

"Legend," according to William Iverson, "has it that when the eagle was selected as our national emblem, the Philadelphia mint adopted a live specimen named Peter, who posed for several early coins before he got tangled up in the mint's machinery." It seems he retained his civil service status. His fellow employees made him one of them and had him stuffed.

The Lincoln, Washington, Jefferson, Franklin Roosevelt, and Kennedy coins were all designed using portraits of these presidents. The Indian on the old cent, it is said, was a real, live person who posed for her picture. Her name was Sarah Longacre, and she was the daughter of an official working at the mint.

BIG-TIME BARTER

The last time barter was used on a national scale was after World War II, when Germany's currency became temporarily worthless.

BEER ON TAB

The Babylonians are credited with thinking up the idea of establishing credit. In ancient times, a barmaid would keep a record of a thirsty customer's drinks on a wet clay tablet. The clay was then baked to form a permanent record. When the grain was harvested at the end of the year, the tablet was passed around for collection. Could this have been the first use of the words, "Put it on my tab"?

THE OLDEST FORM OF MONEY, ALMOST

Shells of a species of mollusk commonly found in the shallow tropical waters of the Indian Ocean were widely used as a form of money in ancient India and Thailand, and in both East and West Africa. When the Chinese writing system was being developed in the second millenium B.C., its inventors and early users considered the cowrie shell the most appropriate symbol for money.

Also used for money were animal hides, cloth, cattle, and slaves.

to buy

to sell

to demand payment

to barter

to trade

BARTERING AS A MEANS OF EXCHANGE

Tea was one of the first commodities used for barter. Historians have established that the cultivation of tea began in Szechwan in China around the year 350 A.D. Even by that time, the Chinese government had a fairly sophisticated system of banking, but minted money was still regarded with considerable suspicion in the rural areas and tea was commonly used as a medium of exchange. It was formed into easily transportable bricks. The further it traveled from the place it was cultivated, the higher the price it commanded.

PENNY-WISE, POUND-FOOLISH

In his book *O the Times, O the Manners!* William Iverson tells us, "Like most primitive peoples, the cattle-keeping Africans originally had but two uses for money: to pay a debt of 'blood money' to the relatives of one's victims and to purchase wives. A girl in the medium-price range went for three cows and a bull, though most fathers were open to any reasonable deal and prices were scaled to the year and model."

IN THE BEGINNING

Some insist that the first coins were made during the seventh century B.C. in Lydia, a country that now forms the western part of Turkey. However, other historians think the idea of coins as a means of exchange was developed simultaneously in China and India. Until coins were developed, the Chinese people bartered usable metal tools such as knives and spades. Gradually, these tools were miniaturized and made into replicas. It was these minitools that evolved into coins.

SALT FOR HIRE

The Romans exchanged salt for work, and from this origin is derived our word "salary." Bartering goods for services, or exchanging one commodity for another, has always been a popular way of avoiding the tax collectors. Among the many popular items for barter have been rattlesnake rattles, iron nails, dried salt cod, and tobacco. In Hawaii, in early times, a fishhook commanded a higher trading value if it was sunk into a just-caught fish. As any starving artist knows, a painting may be offered in exchange for root canal work, if the dentist is a person of culture and a collector of art.

ONLY TIME WILL TELL

A contributor to *Rules of Thumb* reports, "The number of minutes you will wait in line at the bank is equal to the number of people ahead of you divided by the number of tellers times 2.75."

PAPER POWER

China is thought to be the first country to develop paper money, evolved from bark, as a means of exchange. The paper bills were rather quaintly known as bank notes. These notes were issued by the banks as well as by private institutions and companies before it dawned on governors and governments that they should be the ones in charge.

STRINGING THEM ALONG

North American Indians took beads made from shells and threaded them together into belts, necklaces, or bracelets. The wearer of this wampum could thus have on hand his ready "cash." Having a lot of strings of wampum probably entitled the bearer to a little credit too.

The Apaches added another wrinkle to the old ways of doing business. They traded small black stones for horses and rifles. What the Indians did not know, or perhaps did not even care about, was that the "stones" were actually silver.

FRENCH CANADIANS HAVE ALWAYS LOVED TO PLAY

In 1685, when Canada was still a French colony, great difficulty in transporting real money to pay the soldiers who were stationed in Canada necessitated a new means of payment. The solution to the problem was to issue paper money in the form of rather beautiful playing cards. Various suits were assigned differing values. To authenticate them, the governor, representing the king of France (as a sort of pseudo king of diamonds), signed the back of every card.

PRAISE THE LORD

Winston Churchill comments, in his *History of the English-Speaking Peoples,* that the first British denominations of money were exact replicas of coins from the Middle East. Many years passed before the discovery that the translation of the pretty design on the coins declared, "There is but one God, and that God is Allah." One supposes there must have been quite a crusade to recall the merchandise.

DOLLAR

CORNERING THE MARKET

The wily British refused to allow the American colonies to mint their own money. Instead, British currency was, theoretically, the only legal tender. This control of the purse strings enabled Britain to maintain a monopoly and prevented the colonies from trading with any other countries.

IN GOD WE TRUST

The Civil War generated a considerable amount of religious fervor, so much so that Salmon P. Chase, who was then Secretary of the Treasury, authorized the use of the motto "In God We Trust" in 1864. The Chase face appears on the $10,000 bill.

An engraved rendering of John Trumbull's painting of the signing of the Declaration of Independence appears on the back of the $2 Federal Reserve note. We trust in God—and the Federal Reserve Bank ensures that our trust is well placed.

MULTI-USE OPERATIONS

Laundering used to be done in big tubs by strong-armed women slapping sudsy clothes against a washboard. These days, the washing machine does it all for us, using detergent instead of soap. Procter & Gamble, which sells not a little detergent, notes that a family of four launders about a ton of household items and clothing a year.

Money laundering—unlike household laundering—is still done the old-fashioned way: pay dirt from a source the recipient would definitely prefer not to discuss is put into a "legitimate" business over which the recipient also has control (though not always under his own name). It is subsequently withdrawn in whatever legal form he prefers. The payments covering his profits, royalties, or salary can appear on the business' books, seemingly without taint, and the actual dollar bills they represent return to circulation with a new identity, much like children's clothing after summer camp. But, in fact, the dollars have ring around the collar.

PIN MONEY

In the late 15th century, a husband customarily gave a silver pin to his wife in recognition of services rendered. In time, these tokens became known as pin money. Did the wife pawn the pins for real money, we wonder?

DURABLE GOODS

A dollar bill has a life of about nine months. It won't last any longer even if it is laundered. If you tear the dollar though and have both pieces, the bank will exchange the damaged note for a new one.

MAKING IT LAST FOREVER

Keep an eye out for anyone who has dropped a billion one-dollar bills. If you picked up the bills at the rate of one a second, eight hours a day, for a five-day week, it would take 134 years to gather them all.

NOW YOU SEE IT, NOW YOU DON'T

Bills of denominations over $500 are removed from circulation when they fall into the hands of the Federal Reserve Bank.

THE SUBWAY DOES NOT STOP HERE

First, we need to know that a gold brick is about the same size and shape as a brick brick. Each brick weighs about 400 troy ounces. (They are not, surprisingly, all exactly the same weight.) To imagine the heft of this brick in your hand, consider that 400 troy ounces is about 27 pounds, or the weight of a two-year-old child. Each brick is worth about $17,000.

Next, if you want to know where to find a heap of gold bricks, the largest number of them are tucked safely away 80 feet beneath the ground in the Wall Street district of New York. Tourists are allowed to visit the gold. No samples are given away.

INSTANT GRATIFICATION

In 1987, we used plastic cards to charge purchases amounting to $374 billion.

"Polly wants a 1969 dollar!"

CHANGING HANDS

A money exchanger customarily sits behind impenetrable steel bars, though she can get up and leave any time she wishes. She knows the precise value of many currencies, including the Afghanistan *afghani*, the *balboa* (Panamanian money), and the *colon*, which is what is used for money in El Salvador. In Southern Yemen, the money used is the *dinar*; Haiti deals in *gourdes*; in Laos they use *kips*; in Zambia, the *kwacha*; and if you go to Poland, you will need to secure a supply of *zlotys*.

CHECKING IT OUT

The Federal Reserve Board reports that consumers use cash for 35 percent of all purchases, checks for 60 percent, and credit cards for only 6 percent of the things we think we need.

DOING IT THE HARD WAY

The goal for almost every industry is to find easier ways to manufacture its products, but when the product is the printing of money, the objective is the opposite. Here the focus is on developing more and more intricate and complicated procedures so that a counterfeiter will not be able to come even close to the genuine thing.

Highly skilled artists, whose medium is bank notes, create unique geometric designs, scrolls and distinctive letters and numbers, which are preserved, down to the tiniest detail in the engraving process. The counterfeiter does not have the original art to copy, so he must use a photograph of the money as his model. At best, the results will deceive only an inattentive person and with the most sophisticated technology the counterfeiter cannot match the quality of the ink or the paper of a true bill; the authentic bank note has a recognizable, familiar feel and strength to it. The life of the counterfeit note is usually short and the life of the counterfeiter eventually leads to one of long contemplation in confined quarters.

Following are guidelines set forth by the Federal Reserve Bank for spotting a counterfeit:

SEAL

GENUINE

Saw-tooth points around rim are even and sharp.

COUNTERFEIT

Saw-tooth points may be uneven. blunt, or broken

PORTRAIT

GENUINE

Stands out sharply from background. Eyes appear lifelike. Background is a fine screen of regular, unbroken lines.

COUNTERFEIT

May merge with background. Eyes, etc., may be dull or smudgy. Background may be dark, with some irregular and broken lines. Face may seem unnaturally white.

SERIAL NUMBERS

GENUINE

Figures are firmly and evenly printed, well spaced. On Federal Reserve Notes, prefix letter always agrees with District letter in seal.

COUNTERFEIT

May be out of line, poorly spaced, printed too light or too dark. Prefix letter may not agree with District letter in seal.

SCROLL WORK

GENUINE

Fine crisscrossing lines are sharp and unbroken.

COUNTERFEIT

Lines may be blurred and are often broken.

SECURITY FOR THOSE WHO FEAR AND EVEN THOSE WHO HAVE PAID THEIR BILLS ON TIME

As you know, all countries have their own monetary system and the Vatican, being an independent state, is no exception. Should you decide to bank with the Pope, there is a place just for you: Banco di Santo Spirito, Rome. The staff are all very spritely, and their financial advice is visionary.

DON'T BOTHER TO SIGN, JUST PRESS HERE

Thumb prints are the hottest thing in the identification game. We are fast approaching the time when all business will be conducted with the thumb. In order to pay for dinner, a car, an education, or a haircut, you will be required to press the all-important thumb onto a computer-connected console. The computer will automatically deduct the funds from your bank account or offer you alternative means of credit. You will never be able to escape. Once you have used up your credit limit, your thumb will become nonoperational.

CREDIT CARDS MAY SOON BECOME OBSOLETE

For security reasons, many new electronic devices are being used. We have heard that certain doors will open only when you place your eye close to an optical scanner. If your eye print matches your on-record identification, you may enter. In other cases, access will be permitted by voice print or the punching of a code number into a console. Once you have gained entry, if you decide to make any purchases—to buy lunch, for example—you will be given a credit card with which to get hot or cold food from a vending machine. Future generations may never actually see either money or keys. All transactions will be made electronically.

A father is a banker provided by nature.

PROVERB

RAKING IT IN

Hundreds upon thousands of times, we have heard inspiring stories about those who have risen from the ashes and touched the stars. We never weary of these tales even though we sometimes suspect the truth to be less than absolute.

THINGS NOT LEARNED
IN BUSINESS SCHOOL

Andrew Carnegie was already earning by the age of 12. He received $1.20 a week working as a mill hand. When he was 62, he pocketed $500 million when he sold his steel company.

A MAN FOR ALL TIMES

John D. Rockefeller was only 16 when he made his first major contribution to a cause in which he believed. In 1935, his vision seemed to promise the triumph of America over the hard times of the Depression. He provided work for the 75,000 workers who built the Rockefeller Center, with its silvery towers that scrape the sky. The building came to symbolize the nation's faith in its future.

By the time he died, at the age of 82, Rockefeller had fulfilled many dreams for many people—and had given away $531,326,842. The philanthropy of the Rockefellers continues into the third and fourth generation.

SOME DAYS YOU GET
THE PEANUTS

In early 1987, Terry Williams went to Reno, Nevada. He left Reno having won the largest slot machine payoff ever, $4.9 million. His favorite song? "I Am a Gambling Man."

THE KEYS TO SUCCESS

C. Northcote Parkinson, of Parkinson's Law fame, hands on some cautionary words. "There are," he says, "three typical causes of disaster. First is the confusion of purpose. A second cause of possible disaster lies in overgenerous investment. Up to a certain point, the injection of capital produces good results. Beyond that point, the whole process goes into reverse. A third cause of disaster results from a mistake in timing. A good idea can be put forward some fifty years too late. A still better idea can be advocated some twenty years too soon. Even five years either way can be fatal. Our tendency, next time, is to do the reverse of what we did before, each mistake being followed by its opposite."

NICKELS AND DIMES

Frank Woolworth has a tale to top most other Horatio Algers; his rise was meteoric. In 1874, when working as a dry-goods clerk in a general store, he gathered together a group of small items, put them on a tray, marked them down to either 5 or 10 cents, and sold the lot by the end of the day. Six years later, he owned a chain of 25 stores, with annual sales of over a million bucks, all of them coming to the cash register priced at a nickel or a dime.

TAKING THE FIFTH AMENDMENT A LITTLE LATE

William R. Doyle wanted to impress his friends by telling them how much money he had. The only problem with this form of bragging was that the Internal Revenue Service heard about it and billed Doyle $104.2 million in back taxes plus interest. Unfortunately, Doyle had been lying all along. He was penniless.

Go tell that to the judge.

The secret of moneymaking is to care for nothing else and to work at nothing else.

GEORGE BERNARD SHAW

ON THE FLOOR

Bob Tamarkin describes a commodity trader as "a street fighter in a capitalist ghetto." "But," he adds, "where else can you make $50, $100, $500, $1,000 on one lungful of air?"

IS THIS ALL THERE IS?

E. Sterling Hunsaker is the king of debt. When he declared bankruptcy in 1981, his total liabilities amounted to two-thirds of the federal debt. The government asked him to pay $613 billion.

Mr. Hunsaker declined.

Beware of people who say they're going to invest your money as if it were their own— pretty soon it is!

ROBERT ORBEN

Never invest your money in anything that eats or needs repairing.

BILLY ROSE

CRIME DOES NOT PAY. OR DOES IT?

The average take by a bank robber is only $3,000. This translates into 10 banks for a Mercedes and 5 for a good lawyer. The average amount stolen by pickpockets per incident is $218, unless their victim has just robbed a bank.

It was estimated by the magazine of the Conference Board that "the American Mafia would net $30 billion in profits on gross receipts of $50 billion in 1987." Wharton Econometrics estimates that a bona fide Mafia member will have an average annual (tax-free) take-home pay of $250,000.

That could buy a lot of spaghetti dinners.

IDEAS THAT SELL

A better mousetrap, the electric toaster, contact lenses, the zipper, the button, cigarettes, the six-pack, the electric light bulb, Tupperware, soda, potato chips, the VCR, car telephones, *Gone With the Wind,* ice cubes, Mickey Mouse, the aerosol can, Vallum, kitty litter, air travel, underarm deodorant, floppy disks, and paper tissues.

Things that don't sell: advice, *ginzu* knives, and fruitcake.

JUST GIVE ME A VOWEL

Forty-three million people watch the game show "Wheel of Fortune" every day, identifying vicariously with the thrill of seeing money (and cars) falling from the skies.

BEING BAD IS GOOD FOR SOMETHING

Michael Tyson earned $22 million in a minute and a half. His record earnings can be approached only by another Michael—Michael Jackson. The lyrics to his songs rarely consist of more than a few words and yet his BAD album has sold more than 15 million copies worldwide since its release in August of 1987. And that ain't bad.

ON THE NOSE

Michael Tyson, the heavyweight boxing champion, has perhaps fulfilled the ultimate American dream, going from reform school to earning $140,000 a second for 91 seconds in the ring on June 28, 1988. There is a down side though. The *Journal of the American Medical Association* says that 87 percent of professional boxers sustain brain damage as a result of boxing.

If little kids don't aspire to make money like I did, what the hell good is this country?

LEE IACOCCA

MORE LILIES IN THE FIELD

Forbes used various sources, including *Amusement Business, Video Marketing Newsletter,* and *Variety,* to obtain the following information: in 1987 William H. Cosby Jr. earned $57 million; Sylvester Stallone grossed $21 million to arrive at a two-year total income of $74 million; and Bruce Springsteen acquired $56 million in that same time period. Others did less well. Michael Jackson scooped up only $31 million last year—but then he's still young. Johnny Carson took home, before taxes, $20 million for a year's work, and Phil Donahue and Oprah Winfrey reaped $8 million each for talking to millions about subjects that would have shocked our grandparents.

A rich man is nothing but a poor man with money.

W. C. FIELDS

"Give or take a billion tax dollars,
of course."

BUT THE TAXES ARE HIGH TOO

For forecasting the weather on NBC's "Today Show," wishing folks a happy 100th birthday, and giving some talks and endorsements, Willard Scott accumulated $1,900,000 in 1987.

For discussing current issues on television, Ted Koppel earned $1,700,000. This amount did not, however, command total respect from George Bush who, when interviewed by Ted, insisted on calling him—Dan.

For providing the nation's youth with playthings, the chief executive officer of Toys "R" Us, Charles Lazarus, takes home $60 million.

For being good at figures and having the ability to figure things out too, the chief executive officer of the Lotus Corporation, Jim P. Manzi, was the highest paid worker in the nation, earning some $26 million.

Lee Iacocca didn't do too badly in 1987 either. He earned close to $18 million. Asked about the disparity between his paycheck and Manzi's he noted, "Manzi is another Italian boy. I gotta write him a letter." We bet it won't contain a job offer though.

FOR LOVE AND MONEY

The Harper's Index Book, a treasure trove of useful data, has provided us with the startling information that a mere 16 percent of American men who earn less than $5,000 a year admit to cheating on their wives. Among the group earning $70,000 and more, a whopping 70 percent claim to be cheating on their wives. There are no reports on the women's role in this. Do you suppose the women selected by the big earners are the wives of similar big earners, or are they the wives of those who are earning less than $5,000 a year?

If you can actually count your money, then you're not a really rich man.

PAUL GETTY

FAST WAYS TO MAKE MONEY

''Earn $1,000 a week in your own home. No experience necessary.''

''Live in the country of your dreams tax free. Send $100 for more information.''

''Turn those idle minutes into investing in valuable real estate.''

"You may have won $1,000,000. Open this envelope."

"No medical examination is necessary, even if you are over a hundred."

"Diamond earrings, matching necklace, bracelet, and insert for your front tooth. Send check or money order. Sorry no CODs."

"Your help is urgently needed. Your reward will be found in Heaven."

WOMEN ARE REFUSING TO RETIRE

A radio report caught our attention recently. "A woman," said the voice in our car, "should, according to the national average, be earning $1,000 for each year of her age." There were no comments made about men's earnings.

IT DOESN'T MEAN THE SAME AS ONCE IT DID

Today, there are 2.5 million millionaires living in the United States. There are 129 billionaires living all over the place. Forty percent of all billionaires live in the United States, but the two wealthiest men are both Japanese. One is thought to have assets of $16 billion, and the other is not far behind, with $15 billion.

LADIES' DAYS

For several decades, beginning about 1911, most banking offices maintained a department exclusively for women customers. There they could conduct banking transactions with their own special teller (a man), write business letters, or simply relax. We learned these facts from *American Banker,* which goes on to say, "Although women were allowed to use the main lobby of the bank, it was felt that many of them would be uncomfortable in such a man's world."

The 1988 *Statistical Abstract of the United States* has tabulated that in the period between 1984 and 1985, 14.4 million women had total assets of $148,915,000,000 and a total net worth of $142,935,000,000. We must suppose they did not feel ALL THAT uncomfortable after all.

Never let a man jeopardize a fortune that he has earned in a legitimate way, by investing it in things in which he has no experience.

P. T. BARNUM

WOMEN'S BANKS ARE NOT AS NEW AS WE THOUGHT

La Veuve Clicquot (an endearment of sorts meaning the Widow Clicquot) was a woman of high resolve, born in Reims, France in 1777. In 1796, before she had reached her 20th birthday, she became the widow of a highly successful champagne shipper. With enormous difficulty and despite considerable anti-feminist prejudice, she continued to operate the thriving company. Fast off the mark after the Napoleonic Wars, she ran the naval blockade to ship champagne to the Russians, who had developed a mighty thirst for her particular, distinctive sparkling wine. The Russians at first refused to accept shipments claiming, honorably, that they had no funds with which to pay for their purchases. No problem. *La Veuve* promptly opened a bank to serve their interests and hers. She died a wealthy woman.

On October 6, 1919 another woman, Brenda Runyon, the wife of a Nashville physician, founded The First Women's Bank of Clarksville, Tennessee. Opening with a capitalization of $15,000 and an all-female staff, the bank brought in deposits of $20,000 on the first day of business. Eventually, in 1926, after Mrs. Runyon sustained a serious injury, her bank was merged with First Trust & Savings Bank.

The First Women's Bank of New York was opened in 1975. Mr. Martin Simon is Chief Operating Officer and Chairman of the Board of this venture.

TAKING A CHANCE

Joseph Jagger was an expert on spindles, the kind that are used on roulette wheels. A man of keen observation, he noticed that the spindle on a roulette table was not turning smoothly. He studied its movements for a week. Using the laws of probability and his knowledge of the workings of spindles, he placed his bets accordingly, and that was how he came to be known as the man who broke the bank in Monte Carlo.

When I was young, I used to think that money was the most important thing in life; now that I am old, I know it is.

OSCAR WILDE

CHAPTER 4

WORTH
EVERY PENNY

The teacher asked the children to draw a dime. A rich kid drew one that was tiny—about half of the size of a real dime. A poor child drew the dime as big as the moon. How we view money may have very little to do with whether we are rich or poor. Neither does how we spend money: the poor are often more willing to spend than the rich folk. Some people like to spend and others prefer to save.

But, in the final analysis, the rain rains on rainy days for everyone equally.

WHERE IT GOES

The International Council of Shopping Centers has been doing a lot of counting. The organization says that $584 billion is the number of dollars we spent in 1987 in the nation's 30,000 shopping malls.

THE CREAM OF THE CROP

The Holstein-Friesian Association of America reports the most money paid so far for a Holstein at auction is $1,450,000. Why so much? Each ovum can be sliced into eight parts, and the little offspring will multiply mightily across the land too.

SOME SECONDHAND CARS HAVE CHARISMA

Robert Gottleib, editor of *Motor Trend,* says, ''Ever since the October 19 stock market crash, we've seen a surge of investors buying old cars.''

''An old car,'' says one who is addicted to the hobby, is a ''mechanical work of art.'' A 1931 Duesenberg recently fetched the astronomical price of $650,000. No report is available as to whether you can actually drive it on a Sunday afternoon, nor are there any plans to bring back the Edsel.

COUNTRY SEATS ARE SWINGING

New York magazine reports that Ralph Lauren is adding to his 200-acre, $21 million estate, a two-story 30-car garage to provide shelter for his collection of Ferraris. Lauren declined comment on the story. "Whose life is it anyway?" he did not ask.

THE WORM TURNS

The National Gardening Association advises that if you spend $41 to plant a 325 square-foot garden, you may confidently expect to reap $260 worth of vegetables.

Backache remedies have not been added to this figure.

THE VIEW IS BETTER UNOBSTRUCTED

An apartment sale was reported in 1988. The location was the Trump Parc. The purchaser, a Japanese businessman. What was purchased? Seven adjoining three-bedroom apartments. That added up to 21 bedrooms.

Now there are either no bedrooms or one, depending on how you look it. The new owner's first step after approving the space was to knock down all the walls. He now has a very large, one-room apartment. The purchase price was $21 million. The demolition added another couple of million.

A LICENSE TO SELL

In 1988, Quaker Oats paid $25 million to use the characters from the movie *Willow*. Make-believe characters can, it seems, make believers out of us.

The Licensing Letter, reports that licensing revenues in 1987 fell to $2.2 billion from a 1985 high of $3.5 billion. Nevertheless, we can expect to see everything we touch decorated with a parade of cartoon characters. Alligators, dinosaurs, and tigers too have had their moment in the sun. Meanwhile, Goldilocks and the three bears are still eating their porridge in a small clearing in a small forest as they did once upon a time.

RESTING COMFORTABLY

The most expensive private room at the New York Hospital—Cornell Medical Center is $825 a day. (The night is included in this figure.)

SLEEP TIGHT

To spend one night in the triplex suite at the Helmsley Palace Hotel costs $2,000. If you go to sleep at midnight and wake up at seven in the morning, it works out to $4.76 a minute.

A breakfast of orange juice, two fried eggs, bacon, and coffee will cost $23.16 plus the tip.

THE COST OF HIGH LIVING

If you can't get it wholesale, the American Fur Industry tells us that the retail cost of a full-length mink coat is between $7,000 and $10,000. For a sable, expect to tell your friends that you—or a loved one—paid $40,000 to $80,000.

One reason we have heard for wanting to own a fur coat: "When I am asked if I am going to wear my fur tonight, I usually say no. Now that I have one, I don't need to wear it. Before, I didn't have the choice."

NOT ALL ART IS FINE

A chimpanzee artist by the name of Betsy likes to "finger-paint." The highest price paid for one of her works is $75. Still, sometimes it's volume that counts.

I WOULD DRIVE
DOWN THE AVENUE, BUT. . .

In *Quest,* a magazine of costly residential properties and country estates, the following for-sale notice was spotted:

WESTPORT—ONE OF A KIND

Baronial estate in the Spanish style on 2 3/4 totally secluded acres. Indoor pool with spa. Wine cellar. 5 bedrooms in main house. Guest house with bedroom, bath, exercise room, enormous professional woodworking shop. Could be converted to corporate office. Dance/music, or artist's studio. Stone lakefront cabana. Rooftop terrace and rock garden. Multi fish ponds. Tennis court. River with waterfall. Lake. Manicured and magnificently landscaped gardens. $6,000,000.

We wondered what the present owners are up to in the woodworking shop. Do you suppose they are whittling wooden nickels?

BAD NEWS AT
THE FISHING HOLE

The summer drought of 1988 had more than the obvious casualties. The ground was so dry that the night crawlers—the preferred fishing bait—burrowed deeper in their search for moisture and couldn't make it to the surface in time for the nightly roundups. Those that did make it were so scarce, the per-dozen price in Hamburg, New York, escalated to $1.49.

GOING BROKE ISN'T CHEAP

Getty Oil Company had agreed to be purchased by Pennzoil. Texaco stepped in with a sweeter offer. Pennzoil, the rejected suitor, then sued Texaco. Texaco was assessed $10.53 billion in damages when this company stepped up to buy Getty after a gentleman's agreement had purportedly been previously reached.

To sort out who said what to whom, 19 law firms entered the case. Their total bill amounted to 10,594,058 dollars and 75 cents. Even forgetting the 75 cents, talk doesn't come cheap either.

Said Harold Jones, the federal bankruptcy trustee, "I don't think the fees were in any way, shape, or form out of line." Harold Jones is a lawyer too.

CAREER CURVES HAVE CHANGED

Mothers, on hearing the news, snatched the tennis rackets from the hands of their small children and gave them brushes: $53.9 million was the price paid in 1987 at Sotheby's for van Gogh's *Irises;* in the same year, Christie's in London sold the artist's *Sunflowers* for $39.9 million and *The Bridge of Trinquetaille* for $20.2 million. In 1985, van Gogh's *Landscape With Rising Sun* was a real steal at a mere $9.9 million.

WHEN HARVARD CALLS, ALUMNI ANSWER

Alumni coughed up $360 million as a result of a recent fund-raising drive. Harvard is 350 years old, so this figure amounts to a million for every year and some left over to wish upon.

BEFORE DEPARTING

If you would like to endow a chair at Yale University, it will run you about $1,500,000. To commemorate your name at Harvard will cost the same amount. Heed Oliver Wendell Holmes and ''Learn to give/ Money to colleges while you live.''

ROOMS WITH A VIEW

If you don't mind a small space and if money is no object, there are plenty of apartments available in New York City. A one-bedroom apartment was sold, before the Crash of 1987, for $1,175,000. Monthly maintenance costs are extra.

A center box containing eight seats at the Metropolitan Opera will entitle you to see nine performances and will cost $7,056 for the season. If you are content with a view off to one side, a box can be had for a mere $4,536.

THANKS FOR THE MEMORY

Retail stores are cheering. There is a stampede to the altar, and the figures are showing a big increase in the number of weddings, particularly big, splashy formal weddings. *Brides* magazine forecasted that "in 1988 alone, the bridal market will generate $24 billion in retail sales." This news is heartwarming for manufacturers of toaster ovens, bath mats, kitchen tools, beds, and silverware. It is also good news for jewelry stores. A wedding band can cost anywhere from $100 for a gold band to $100,000 for a be-jewelled eternity ring. Little things sometimes cost a lot.

The cost of the wedding ceremony itself is, though, surprisingly modest, considering its importance. Loving couples can expect to pay between $10 and $100 for a 15-minute ceremony.

Unloving couples can count on paying between $250 and $350 an hour for the services of a fancy divorce lawyer. It takes many more hours to dissolve a marriage than to make one.

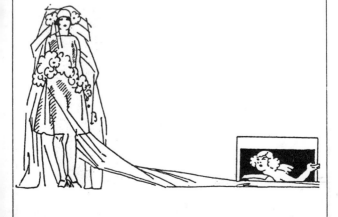

READING BETWEEN THE LINES

In America we spend—give or take an issue or two—$5 billion on magazines every year. Magazines survive, however, not on the reader subscriptions, though they certainly help, but on the advertisers' messages.

- A full-page color ad in the *New Yorker* is $20,820 if the person placing the ad is a publisher; mere mortals have to pay $25,985 to reach the select and highly desirable readership of this magazine.
- A similar ad in *Time* costs $120,130. *Time* has many more readers than the *New Yorker.*
- *According to Advertising Age,* the cost for a full-page color ad in *New Women* for September 1988 in a Great American Designers special fashion issue is $21,620.
- In *Working Woman's* fall fashion portfolio, the equivalent ad costs $26,700.
- In *Vogue,* it is $31,200 + 15% for bleed and in *Lears* (a magazine for the woman who was not born yesterday), it is $10,375.

BEAUTY IS IN THE
EYE OF THE BEHOLDER

When Lisa Gherardini (whose portrait is known as the Mona Lisa) showed her husband Leonardo's effort, he hated it and refused to buy it. It is now considered the most valuable painting in the world.

Gertrude and Leo Stein paid Picasso $30 for his painting, *Girl With Basket of Flowers.* It was the best, and only, offer he got at the time. Things picked up for him later.

IT WAS NIP AND TUCK
ALL THE WAY

James Hirsch, writing in *The New York Times* in June 1988, uncovered the following fascinating facts and figures: 100,000 liposuction operations were performed last year at a per-operation cost of between $500 and $4,000—depending on how many lips there are, perhaps? Eye lifts cost between $1,000 and $4,000.

We have always wondered: if you remove 10 or 15 years from your body, does your mind stay the same, regress proportionately, or compensate proportionately?

PUT YOURSELF IN
THE DRIVER'S SEAT

- Rolls Royce Silver Spur limousine, $198,000
- Aston Martin Lagonda Saloon, $187,500
- Lamborghini, $150,000
- Ferrari Testarossa, $135,000
- Jaguar XJ-S convertible, $52,000

OTHER HIGH-PRICED SEATS

An avid 21,785 boxing fans paid up to $1,500 to sit on folding chairs and watch the Tyson-Spinks 91-second fight. In addition, untold millions paid rental fees of up to $50 to watch the fight on PPV ("pay-per-view") cable home TV channels. That was the fight in which Spinks, earned $13.5 million for just getting up and lying down three times.

TIED IN KNOTS

It is difficult to find an explanation for the phenomenon. Every day, millions of businessmen are unable to leave the house without first tying a length of colored fabric around their necks. For a decent-looking piece of cloth, the price ranges from a dollar or two up to a hundred.

To go with the tie, a smart wool suit from the designer Luciano Barbera costs in the neighborhood of $1,500.

HOLDING MOST, IF NOT ALL, THE CARDS

Donald Trump said recently, unsmilingly, that he thought it good for the United States to bring things into the country instead of seeing them leave our shores. With this patriotic purpose in mind, he bought, for $30 million, from Adnan Khashoggi, a yacht. He named her the Trump Princess and promptly discovered, as is customary with princesses, that she needed another $10 million to become shipshape.

The ship was launched on Independence Day 1988. She carries a crew of 31 in addition to galaxies of guests. She can hold, says Trump, enough food for 100 people for three months. Should a guest wish to request room service from another commissary, he can use one of the 210 telephones that Mr. Trump has thoughtfully provided.

ROBIN HOOD, WHERE ARE YOU NOW THAT WE NEED YOU?

In January 1987, the United States government spent $84 billion. The Treasury Department reveals that 26 percent of the total amount was spent on national defense. There was a time when government promised us guns and butter. Today, few of us want either, thank you.

LET'S HOPE THE CLOUDS HAVE SILVER LININGS

The Cunard Line doesn't exactly advertise this, but you may be interested to know that if you would like to have your daughter's wedding on board, you can cruise in the Queen Elizabeth 2 overnight, for $500,000.

THE HOT SEAT

The New York Times reports that the price of a seat on the New York Stock Exchange has risen from an average of $207,000 in June 1964 to $1 million in 1988.

The actress Lillian Russell attracted [similar] crowds whenever she took a spin on her bicycle, given her by the ever-generous Diamond Jim Brady. This unusually elegant velocipede had handlebars inlaid with mother-of-pearl, while the spokes of its wheels must have twinkled and flashed in a most eye-catching way, considering that they were encrusted with diamonds, sapphires, rubies, and emeralds. When on tour and covering distances too great for pedaling, so that she had to travel by train, the prudent comedienne would keep her bicycle safe on the journey in a specially designed traveling case made of the finest Moroccan leather.

DAVID FROST'S BOOK OF MILLIONAIRES,
MULTIMILLIONAIRES, AND REALLY RICH PEOPLE

WALK SLOWLY, PLEASE

An artist friend comments that diamonds should not be given in a box. Instead, he believes, so precious a gift should be wrapped in a silk scarf or cloth of gold. David Frost, in another anecdote, tells us that Mr. Gordon Selfridge, of the family of the famous London store, had a similar idea. He gave a gift of a pair of four-karat diamonds to two sisters whom he greatly admired. His gift wasn't put in a box either. He arranged with Cartier to have the matching diamonds mounted in the shells of two matching tortoises. The sisters didn't wear their diamonds. Instead they took them for a (slow) walk.

SAFE SEX—BY CREDIT CARD

Dial-a-Porn is a growing business. Calls to the special 900 numbers that purvey sexually explicit "fantasies" to those prepared to pay by credit card grossed $152 million in the first six months of 1988. Of this, $75 million went into the pockets of the telephone companies. As they say, time is money!

A GOLDEN HANDSHAKE

Walter Monkton was one of the Duke of Windsor's servants. As such, he worked without salary for 20 years. On his retirement, he was rewarded with a cigarette case on which his engraved name was spelled incorrectly. Whether or not he smoked, we may suppose that he fumed.

LITTLE LUXURIES TO EASE THE PAIN

One pound of gorgeous chocolates from Teuscher is $36.

———

Dried mushrooms—morels—are selling, though not briskly, in New York City for $800 a pound, while the humbler dried porcini go for a mere $250. Thieves may be better off going for the fungus and forgetting about what may be in the cash register.

It is easier to praise poverty than to bear it.

PROVERB

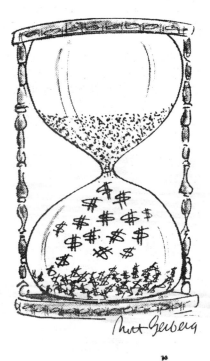

POINTS OF REFERENCE

NEWSPAPERS AND MAGAZINES

Advertising Age
American Banker
Brides
Forbes
Fortune
Holstein World
The Journal of the American
   Medical Association
The Licensing Letter
Manhattan, Inc.
Money

Motor Trend
New Women
New York
The New York Times
People
Quest
Self
Time
The Wall Street Journal
Working Woman

BOOKS

Benham's Book of Quotations.
   Gurney Benham. George G. Harrap and Company.
Bonanzas and Fools Gold: Treasures and Dross From the Nuggetizing of Our Lives.
   Phillip Lesley. Acclaim Communications.
David Frost's Book of Millionaires, Multimillionaires, and Really Rich People.
   David Frost. Crown Publishers Inc.
The Executive's Quotation Book.
   James Charlton. St. Martin's Press Inc.
The Great Thoughts.
   George Seldes, comp. Ballantine Books.
The Harper's Index Book.
   Lewis H. Lapham, Michael Pollan, and Eric Etheridge, eds. Henry Holt and Co.

The Hazards of Walking and Other Memos From Your Bureaucrats.
Carol Trueblood and Donald Fenn, eds. Houghton Mifflin Co.
Isaac Asimov's Book of Facts.
Isaac Asimov. Grosset & Dunlap Inc.
Kickers: All the News That Didn't Fit.
John Bohannon. Ballantine Books.
O the Times, O the Manners!
William Iverson. William Morrow & Co., Inc.
The People's Almanac.
David Wallechinsky and Irving Wallace. Doubleday & Co.
Rules of Thumb.
Tom Parker. Houghton Mifflin Company.
The Synonym Finder.
J.I. Rodale. Rodale Press Inc.
*Why Didn't I Think of That?: Everybody's Book of Million-Dollar
Ideas.*
Randy Cohen and Alexandra Anderson. Fawcett Columbine.

OTHER SOURCES

Federal Reserve Bank of Atlanta
Federal Reserve Bank of New York